ne

Nothing But Words

Jean Stevens' poems have appeared in *London Magazine, Stand, The North, Mslexia, Other Poetry, Smoke, Brittle Star, The Frogmore Papers, The High Window* and the *Bridport Prizewinners' Anthology (2016)*, and have been broadcast on BBC Radio 3 and Radio 4. She is a past winner of the Yorkshire Post Poetry Prize and the Leeds Libraries Writing Prize, and has been shortlisted for the Poetry Business Pamphlet Competition and *The Rialto* Poetry Prize.

Her plays have been performed at Derby Playhouse, the Edinburgh Festival, Harrogate Theatre and West Yorkshire Playhouse, and her stand-up comedy script won the Polo Prize at London's Comedy Store.

As a professional actor she has credits for stage, film and television.

jeanstevenspoet.co.uk

About other poetry collections by Jean Stevens

...searching, restless poems, haunted by both darkness and light
Kim Moore

Filmic and beautiful, full of warmth and drama
Kay Mellor OBE

An exciting contemporary voice
Daljit Nagra

Persuasive and deeply moving
The Yorkshire Times

A sure hand
Ian McMillan

For Jean Stevens, love, grief, elegy, longing are insuperable states of mind, as natural as the taking of measured breaths
Steve Whitaker

Also by Jean Stevens

Poetry

Performances (Pica Press 1999)
Undressing in Winter (Matador 2008)
Beyond Satnav (Indigo Dreams Publishing 2016)
Driving in the Dark (Naked Eye Publishing 2018)
Speak to the Earth (Naked Eye Publishing 2019)

Plays

Twockers, Knockers and Elsie Smith (1997)
Journey (1998)
both published by Smith and Kraus, USA

NOTHING BUT WORDS

Jean Stevens

Naked Eye Publishing

© Jean Stevens 2020

All rights reserved

Book design and typesetting by Naked Eye

ISBN: 9781910981115

www.nakedeyepublishing.co.uk

Acknowledgements

Some of these poems were first published in *Dream Catcher*, *Pennine Platform* and *The North*.

NOTHING BUT WORDS

So difficult it is to show the various meanings
and imperfections of words when we have nothing else
but words to do it with.

John Locke

Contents

These days 13
The bird village 14
I knew them 15
Messages 16
If Sylvia Plath were my best friend 17
Connection 18
The path 19
Midnight in claret and blue 20
I still hear Uncle Stan 21
The people who live inside me 22
Superstition 23
On the train 24
Because you asked 25
A reason to sing 26
On the way to Kimberley 27
Noticing my heart 28
Focus 30
If these things should happen 31
Bookmark 32
Not Rubens 33
Passport not needed 34
What is this place? 35
Not in the words of warning 36
Black cat 37
We waited 38
In the balance 39
Shall we talk 40

These days

I dream of climbing the hill
as I once could
when I never gave it a thought.

I think, just one foot, then the other,
but I walk aware of every muscle
and bone, carrying a lifetime's
freight of words said and regretted,
and the weight of words I should have said

intent on the next
rabbit hole or tussock
watching for the depth
of puddles, the trap of mud
the jagged rocks.

I know there's sky and solitude
that sense of being somewhere else
so I have to make this journey
and rebel against the hard path
in the same forced breath
as I give thanks.

The bird village

When we use words
we speak across deep valleys
where meanings drop into a chasm
and join the quarrels of waterfalls

and I think of Kuşköy, the land
above the Black Sea coast and its steep
climb over pine-covered mountains
where water has cut a deep ravine
and separated families and friends.

No ordinary message carries,
but this is the village of birds
where the people have a language
of whistled Turkish that travels
over the mountains and valleys.

Words, slippery at best, are swallowed
by their ambiguous selves
but the subtle meanings of Kuşköy
fly miles across the divide.

Men and women speak, argue, make love
in whistles. At weddings, their notes mellow
to music and, as we all wish we could,
they sing like birds.

I knew them
    after Mimi Khalvati

Floods made a sog of everything,
but, perched on a twig at the top of a drowning bush,
a wren sang loud from her tiny throat,
and that will do.

You walked up the hill, were taken by mist
going forever out of reach,
but I learned to turn loneliness to solitude,
and that will do.

Mental health doctors shook doleful heads,
but the child I love found worlds of her own
running wild through the woods,
and that will do.

Three friends died in the space of two months,
but I celebrate the words we shared
for I knew them, I knew them, I knew them,
and that will do.

When a homeless man in Leeds held out his cap
I burst into selfish tears,
but he took me into a caff, bought me a cup of tea,
and that will more than do.

Messages

The rich song of blackbirds
and the virtuoso of wrens
welcome early morning and, as evening
deepens, starlings loop the loop across the sky
and the notes and patterns they weave
are the language of fragrant buddleia

the language of rainbowed water
in mist, rain, ice and snow
the language of cello and flute
of canto and madrigal
the language of colour
from the flaunt of red to the cool of green

the language vital for living
at one with the elements.
Our instinct is blunted, worn down
by dishonest words and signs.
Theirs is a language whose meaning
we began to ignore long ago.

If Sylvia Plath were my best friend
           after Nina Mingya Powles

In silence we'd walk up to Wuthering Heights.
She'd be edgy as sheep protecting lambs.
Her nostrils would twitch at smells
my nose couldn't pick out.
She'd feel thistles and thorns to the bone
and see signs of death in everything
at the same time as lusting for life.

Looking down on the narrow, black valley,
she'd give me that girlie talking-to
as we hovered at the edge.

She'd take me to New York
and we'd bury the past in Central Park
be queens of the world drinking champagne
at the top of the Empire State
and we'd say *To hell with men
let's devote our lives to words.*

One day reality would set in.
But I wouldn't be able to tell her
that, although she helped me
find phrases for the dark, not one
of my words could help her at all.

Connection

I didn't learn your number
it's on speed dial and in my memory card.

I can't bring myself to press *delete*;
it would be as if you never were

so I'm keeping the connection
though words are now lost between us.

For such a long time, I thought about,
should have, would have …

and now, when you're no longer here,
I find I know your number by heart.

The path

The hill was high and steep. I longed for sky
then there it was, full of the milk
of loaded clouds, and I thought
of him carrying his burden, my father,
his work-worn hands heavy with
love as he trudged up the difficult slope.

I hoped he'd turn round for one last look and
spell me a route that might lead to the light
but he kept his eyes on the path.

Midnight in claret and blue

I run down the tunnel and onto the pitch
unlit and eerie under the moon
I always looked down on the action
now I look up at the stands,
they really were stands, we didn't sit then.

All those Saturday afternoons
are lost in the shadows
the rattles, groans and cheers
have been silenced by the dark.

I see ghosts of the heroes.
Watch Stanley Matthews, playing
for Blackpool's visiting team, deftly
weave the ball past everyone.

Remember the chilly walk home with Dad
to a roaring fire, hotpot on the stove,
the wireless voices listing goals,

the magical words: Leyton Orient,
Queen of the South, Crewe Alexandra,
Plymouth Argyle, and the faintest hope
of winning the no-score draw.

I still hear Uncle Stan

Every Christmas the family assembled
in the tiny room behind his shop
with its plantless concrete backyard.

Every year he delivered the same verses,
finished with a catch in his voice, and left the air
full of words: *You are nearer God's heart
in a garden than anywhere else on earth.*

Then he shrank, curled back into himself,
saying nothing, while we exchanged
indulgent glances, and his wife
took charge, moving chairs, passing
sandwiches, telling us where to sit.

Those days he was boring Uncle Stan,
but now I want to know what stirred in him
when he had his moments reciting aloud
his voice full of passion and grief.

The people who live inside me

She often said, my mother,
That's not for the likes of you
and she goes on saying it
even though she's dead,

and other voices keep butting in:

*Don't screw your face up like that,
if the wind changes it'll be permanent
and no-one'll want to marry you.*

*Tread on a nick and you'll marry a brick
Tread on a square and you'll marry a bear.*

*You won't get into the house, love.
Your mum's run off with a tramp.*

*You'd better be a good girl or those lions
outside the town hall will gobble you up.*

And the mesh of the voices that bothered me
blends with what I thought I heard my parents
say in bed on the darkest nights
that puzzled and frightened me

and knits together with all the other words
inside the head of a child who's a grandmother now
yet even more of a child, still trying
to learn the impossible language.

Superstition

The means of fire moved in with me
from the home left behind
when everything changed.

They're safety matches
but from the start they've had
the smell of smoke and charring.

Lost in the past are the open fires,
barbecues, shared cigarettes,
but words of superstition stayed:

Bad things come in threes.
When there've been two,
it's time to create a third yourself.
Strike a match, blow out the flame,
snap the stick in half.

That's the only reason I keep them.
That, or to light the infrequent candle.

On the train

He got on the train
and sat opposite
in shabby jacket
torn jeans
trainers worn into holes.

Words were tucked
in the pocket over his heart.
Metaphors danced round his groin.
Truth flashed in his eyes.

He leaned towards me -
I tried to pick up
the messages and was just
beginning to grasp things

when the poem stood up
and walked past me
got off at Cassiobridge.

Because you asked

I'll tell you.

Every poem simply has to be
begins with a reaching out
has its own pen and creates
the flow of every letter
the mystery of each space.

It adventures
across the whiteness
totally in charge
managing the nothingness
until the pen
the words
and the space
have written me

then, flexing its muscles
into an independent stride,
the poem walks through the world
living its life.

A reason to sing

Carry your shoes from the place of the dead
and walk across the world.

Let your bare feet sift the sand,
squelch the mud, test the stone

till you come to the old blue oak
its roots lifting from the ground

where explorers once travelled
hunting the words you're looking for

and where they found in the dark
a reason to sing.

A reason to sing known to the tiger
when the earth was a different place

not this burnt-out green
stripped bare to the bone.

On the way to Kimberley

I hang in the air above
the Outback's Red Centre
on the way to Kimberley
in a patched-up four-person plane
with hiccups for an engine

and waiting below
is treeless, waterless
featureless burning earth.

No tramlines
no railway stations,
no cars hellbent
for somewhere else,
no lights in huddled apartments,
no road signs to tell me places exist
no anchoring words.

Is this what it's like
to be balanced forever
between the stuttering of my breath
and the place where the trial begins?

Noticing my heart

In the dark, you've been
working hard for years.
I've been a rotten friend
and only notice you now.

When I was a child
did you hop, skip, jump,
pulsate when I met the one,
beat even faster when we made love,

leap with dolphins in the Moray Firth,
hold still in the garden to listen
to thrushes and blackbirds,
contract when I wept by hospital beds,
saw someone lowered into the dark?

How many stops and starts
when I smelt leaking gas,
heard someone move in the shadows,
rode a reckless motorbike?

Deep in my flesh and blood,
ventricles are on go-slow,
atria doing overtime.
I feel veins and valves
jump and reel at random.

When I spoke my poems to a crowd
while wearing a monitor, what lurches
did it record to words like
*Pegasus, galloped, edge of the cliff,
wild and running free?*

I owe you a great big thank you,
hope you can forgive,
while I work out what I'd say
to any other friend
who felt she'd had enough.

Focus

Frozen in the limousine
    in slow procession
        through
            February's skating streets.

She focussed:
    a child dragging a sledge
        a man removing his cap

slippery steps to the porch,
    crystal notes of the choir,
        rustle of order sheets,
            perfume of hyacinths,

a single long-stemmed rose
    floating down into earth,
        the thump of soil on wood,

words crisp on the air,
    the queue of handshakes,
        sandwiches, cups of tea

until the moment
    when everyone
        even her children
            had left
                and returned to their own.

Then the wide, wide bed
    the mobile phone still alive with words
        the jacket hung over the chair.

Because you asked

I'll tell you.

Every poem simply has to be
begins with a reaching out
has its own pen and creates
the flow of every letter
the mystery of each space.

It adventures
across the whiteness
totally in charge
managing the nothingness
until the pen
the words
and the space
have written me

then, flexing its muscles
into an independent stride,
the poem walks through the world
living its life.

A reason to sing

Carry your shoes from the place of the dead
and walk across the world.

Let your bare feet sift the sand,
squelch the mud, test the stone

till you come to the old blue oak
its roots lifting from the ground

where explorers once travelled
hunting the words you're looking for

and where they found in the dark
a reason to sing.

A reason to sing known to the tiger
when the earth was a different place

not this burnt-out green
stripped bare to the bone.

On the way to Kimberley

I hang in the air above
the Outback's Red Centre
on the way to Kimberley
in a patched-up four-person plane
with hiccups for an engine

and waiting below
is treeless, waterless
featureless burning earth.

No tramlines
no railway stations,
no cars hellbent
for somewhere else,
no lights in huddled apartments,
no road signs to tell me places exist
no anchoring words.

Is this what it's like
to be balanced forever
between the stuttering of my breath
and the place where the trial begins?

Noticing my heart

In the dark, you've been
working hard for years.
I've been a rotten friend
and only notice you now.

When I was a child
did you hop, skip, jump,
pulsate when I met the one,
beat even faster when we made love,

leap with dolphins in the Moray Firth,
hold still in the garden to listen
to thrushes and blackbirds,
contract when I wept by hospital beds,
saw someone lowered into the dark?

How many stops and starts
when I smelt leaking gas,
heard someone move in the shadows,
rode a reckless motorbike?

Deep in my flesh and blood,
ventricles are on go-slow,
atria doing overtime.
I feel veins and valves
jump and reel at random.

When I spoke my poems to a crowd
while wearing a monitor, what lurches
did it record to words like
*Pegasus, galloped, edge of the cliff,
wild and running free?*

I owe you a great big thank you,
hope you can forgive,
while I work out what I'd say
to any other friend
who felt she'd had enough.

Focus

Frozen in the limousine
    in slow procession
        through
            February's skating streets.

She focussed:
    a child dragging a sledge
        a man removing his cap

slippery steps to the porch,
    crystal notes of the choir,
        rustle of order sheets,
            perfume of hyacinths,

a single long-stemmed rose
    floating down into earth,
        the thump of soil on wood,

words crisp on the air,
    the queue of handshakes,
        sandwiches, cups of tea

until the moment
    when everyone
        even her children
            had left
                and returned to their own.

Then the wide, wide bed
    the mobile phone still alive with words
        the jacket hung over the chair.

If these things should happen

If you lack a tiger and want one, a tiger you shall have.

If you're starved of love, leave a bucket on the doorstep and love will be delivered with the milk.

Any child who wants to learn from the wild will be guided to the forest by stars, fed by flocks of birds, protected by wolves.

If one of you wants the coldness of snow, the other a blazing sun, you'll be able to walk hand in hand, one in crunching snow boots, the other in strappy sandals, toes tickled by ripening grass.

If you want your own island, then one shall be raised from the seabed overnight.

There'll be a poet on every corner who, if you ask, will be your own minstrel of words.

And, if such is your wish, a cellist shall live in your bones.

If you call upon it to do so, the wall in your room will paint itself like a Rembrandt or a Turner till it's time for you to pass it on.

You can have your own impossible mountain, waves high as the Empire State, your personal South Pole to reach.

If these things should happen, is anything required of you?
Oh, yes.

Bookmark

Slipped between
        two yellowing pages,
the card you sent me
              from Stonehenge.

Was it coincidence
        that at the time
              I was studying Tess's journey
                      to her sleep in the forest of stones,
  and that the card was the last you ever wrote?

Left in a gap myself
        the only thing I find to do
is to take this sprig
        from the rosemary bush you bought me
and leave it here to be preserved.

It marks the words
        where those who were left
             climbed to the top of the hill
and bent to the earth
        remembering.

Not Rubens

With a wet finger someone has pushed
through the grime caked on the back door
of the plumber's van and drawn a nude
with nipples thrust from dumpling breasts,
and smudged the dirt to form her pubic hair.

Though her thighs are plump, she's no Rubens.
Her geometry's too skew-whiff, even
for Picasso. But, on a day so far lacking
sunlight and warmth, she's a cheerful sight:
Eve before the serpent's words.

Passport not needed

When we're finished with words
we'll be fitted with microchips
under our skin with our d.o.b.
address, credit rating,voting habits
and God knows what.

Deeper under our skin, the first breath we took,
the beat of another's heart when we tasted milk,
the first astonishing kiss,
the first time we opened to a lover,
were gifted that ordinary miracle, a child,

the first time we reached the mountain top,
dived down to coral, knelt at the altar,
gave our selves to Housman, Brubeck, Matisse,

the first time someone we loved
dropped out of our lives and into the dark
and God knows what.

What is this place?

What is this place where I fell asleep
this land not asked for?
Where are the roads, the lanes, the tracks?

Were these craters of rubble once houses
are these heaps of cinders and ash
all that remains?

Even the ghosts have left.
There are only things in their absence.

Gone the river's beat
the clip of horses
scratch of brambles and thorns
the sweet-sour taste of berries
the scent in woodland herbs.

Gone the curlew's cry.
Gone all human words.

Not in the words of warning

not in the crash of trees
as the chainsaw grinds
not in the wind barrelling across
a greedy dust bowl

not in the rush of flames
scalping the earth
and leaping miles

not in the choking throats
tasting acrid smoke

not in the waves
making a meal of the land
not in the smell of rotting fish

but, at the far end of the day,
in the fading light,
the quiet stillness
of red deer grazing.

Black cat

Against the blinds
the sun throws shadows
of restless leaves

and for the first time today
the kettle whistles -
a train on its way
to somewhere other than this.

I take my coffee into the garden
and surprise a cat
who's never visited before.

If a black cat
crosses your path
it should bring good luck.

I'll open that envelope soon
risk those black-lettered words.

We waited

grappling with words
firmament and *heaven*
not our place to question

we've bitten the coin of praise
tasted its tainted green

we've waited at the edge of the sea
on railway platforms
in empty houses
for letters that never came
for messages and calls
that seem lost in the air

we have done those things
we ought not to have done

there is no health in us.

In the balance

Queuing with a heavy parcel
for the other side of the world
I shift from leg to leg
when through the window

between a list of Post Office hours
and a poster for Greenpeace
I see a stag standing alone
in the sullen street.

No-one else seems to see him
though he's lit
against the gloom
antlers reaching for the sky.

And I remember the day we walked
past the ruined abbey, the shining water,
the retaining wall, until we came
to uncut grass and unpruned trees
and saw a lone buck grazing.

We watched in the sun
as his red coat flared, and were held
until we returned into time.

Now at the counter, I place the parcel
on the scales, and she tells me
It's going to cost you the earth.

Shall we talk

or shall we go quietly into the evening
drive the route that takes us from home
through tunnels of trees we've seen over the years

remembering stripped branches and twigs
against grey sky, the magic trick of buds
as the days warmed up, flickers of summer sun
through leaves, autumn flares
by the river whose water jousts with rock

come to the old barn restaurant set into the hill
where youngsters bring us plates of plenty
salmon fresh from the local river
potatoes, broccoli, carrots from a hidden garden
and a glass of thank-you wine

till we notice shadows creep over the fields
lights in the valley scattered like confetti
and you walk me to the car

drive back past the old viaduct,
each raised arch as impossible to build
as a circle of standing stones,

and move slowly through the dark
while I weigh the silence
against all those words that might have been.

Naked Eye Publishing

A fresh approach

Naked Eye Publishing is five years in existence and still fledgling: an independent not-for-profit micro-press intent on publishing quality poetry and literature, including in translation. We are also developing a 'Potted Theses' series: academic theses rewritten for the general reader.

A particular focus is translation. We aim to take a midwife role in facilitating the translation of works that have until now been disregarded by English-language publishing. We will be happy if we function purely as an initial stepping-stone both for overlooked writers and first-time literary translators.

Each of us at Naked Eye is a volunteer, competent and professional in our work practice, and not intending to make a profit for the press. We see ourselves as part of the revolution in book publishing, embodying the newly levelled playing field, sidestepping the publishing establishment to produce beautiful books at an affordable price with writers gaining maximum benefit from sales.

nakedeyepublishing.co.uk

www.ingramcontent.com/pod-product-compliance
Lightning Source LLC
Chambersburg PA
CBHW050509120526
44588CB00045B/2297